Made with Love

A collection of recipes handed down
from generation to generation

Compiled by Cindy Elder

DEDICATION

Lovingly dedicated to my daughter Kacey
who brings so much joy into my life.

CONTENTS

Preface

When I was a teenager, Aunt Marge lived close by, so we got together once in a while and became pretty good friends. She taught me of the importance of preserving the past. She even convinced me that if I wrote a letter to Grandpa that I would be pleasantly surprised at the letter I would get back from him. I decided to take her up on the challenge. I still have some of the letters that he wrote to me. I learned a lot about him from those letters and I am grateful that she pushed me a little to do it.

Not too long ago, I came across a stenographer's notebook – you know, the kind with the line down the middle. Aunt Marge had given it to me years ago as a gift. It had 18 recipes in it from Grandma, Great Grandma as well as Aunts and Great Aunts. I had just published a cookbook for my church family and decided it would be fun to preserve these recipes in a published book as well. The only problem was there were not enough recipes to fill a book. Luckily Stuart's Mom, Jan Richardson, had given us copies of her recipes and so I asked other family members to contribute more recipes. This is a compilation of all the recipes I have gathered. Thank you to those of you who contributed to this book. I hope you will treasure the old recipes as much as I do.

APPETIZERS & SNACKS

From the home of
Jan and Owen Richardson

Cheese Ball

1 pkg. cream cheese (8 oz.)
1 small can deviled ham
1 T butter
chopped black olives
chopped nuts

or

1 pkg. cream cheese (8 oz.)
1 small pkg. pimento cheese
1 T butter
chopped black olives
chopped nuts

or

1 pkg. cream cheese (8 oz.)
Roquefort cheese
1 T butter
chopped green olives
chopped nuts

Knead ingredients; heat from hands will melt it together. Add chopped olives. Put in refrigerator until cold enough to form a hard ball.

Roll in nuts and serve.

Easy Hummus

2 cans garbanzo beans, drained
½ C sesame tahini
¼ C lemon juice
2 - 3 cloves garlic
1 tsp. ground cumin
1 tsp. ground coriander
¼ C light vegetable oil
a few drops of toasted sesame oil
2 - 3 T Braggs liquid aminos
salt to taste

Put all ingredients in food processor and blend. Add water until you have the desired consistency.

Add salt to taste.

Optional: Add a small avocado for color and flavor variety.

Note from Jana
Leave who you were, Love who you are,
Look forward to who you will become.
It's time to say hello to the person you've always wanted to be.
The best is yet to come.

From the home of
Jan and Owen Richardson

Crisp Pickle Mix

4 qt. thin sliced cucumbers
1 qt. sliced onions
3 C cauliflower
1 green pepper
3 cloves garlic
½ C coarse salt
5 C sugar
2 T mustard seed
1 ½ tsp. celery seed
1 ½ tsp. turmeric
3 C cider vinegar

Combine vegetables and garlic. Add salt. Cover with ice cubes. Mix well. Let stand 3 hours.

Drain well. Combine remaining ingredients. Pour over vegetables.

Bring just to boiling. Seal in pint jars.

Chill before serving.

Makes 8 - 9 pints.

As with any pickles, make to your taste.

Stuffed Mushrooms

12 large mushrooms
2 T olive oil
½ tsp. salt
¼ tsp. white pepper
2 small stalks celery
1 small shallot or leek
⅛ C chopped parsley
1 oz. shredded cheese
½ oz. grated parmesan
⅛ C dry white wine or low sodium broth
½ C bread crumbs (like Panko)
1 large egg

Preheat oven to 350°.

Clean mushrooms gently. Remove the stems and set aside. Spoon out the gills to make more room for stuffing. Toss the caps in oil, salt and pepper, then arrange stem side up on a rimmed baking sheet.

Chop the stems with the celery, shallots or leeks and simmer in oil over medium-high heat. Season with remaining salt and pepper. Cook until the liquid evaporates and mushroom stems are brown. Remove from pan and set aside.

De-glaze pan: Add wine or broth. Cook until liquid evaporates.

Remove pan from heat and add parsley and bread crumbs. Stir together. Whisk eggs and cheese together and combine with all mixtures. Stuff into caps.

Bake for 20 - 25 minutes or until brown on top.

From the home of
Jan and Owen Richardson

Mustard Pickles

3 qt. small cucumbers, cut
2 or 3 lbs. small onions, chopped
2 heads cauliflower, broken into
bite size pieces
2 large red peppers, chopped
1 ½ C salt
3 qt. apple cider vinegar
1 qt. water
1 C flour
2 ½ C sugar
1 tsp. turmeric
1 tsp. cinnamon
1 tsp. mace
1 tsp. mustard seed
1 T celery seed

Soak cucumbers, onions, cauliflower and red pepper overnight in 1 ½ C salt brine.

Put vinegar, water, sugar and spices in a large pan. Bring to a boil and add vegetables after draining them. Boil 25 minutes.

Add thickening and mustard. Bottle in pint jars.

From the home of
Jana Elder

2 cans of quartered artichoke
hearts, drained
1 can sliced water chestnuts, diced
1 C mayonnaise
1 bag shredded mozzarella cheese
salt, pepper and garlic to taste

Hot Artichoke Dip

Preheat oven to 350°.

Stir all together; add salt, pepper and garlic powder to taste.

Bake for 30 minutes or until top is golden brown.

Serve immediately.

Note from Jana
Great with Triscuits, Wheat Thins and bread. Enjoy!

13

From the home of
Jan and Owen Richardson

Dip for Fruit

1 pkg. lemon pudding
2 C pineapple juice
whipped topping

Make lemon pudding using pineapple juice instead of milk. Mix thoroughly.

Add whipped topping to mixture and serve with fresh fruits of choice.

BREAKFAST

From the home of
Stuart and Cindy Elder

1 orange, peeled and chopped
1 banana, sliced
½ C fresh pineapple tidbits
3 T pecans, chopped
1 T monk fruit sweetener
½ C plain fat free Greek yogurt

Breakfast Fruit Cup

Prepare all fruits as directed and add to a medium size bowl. Stir in yogurt and monk fruit sweetener. Mix thoroughly.

Place each serving into a pretty parfait cup or bowl and sprinkle with pecans on top of each serving.

1 small can of frozen concentrated
orange juice
1 large ripe avocado
5 golden delicious apples or
enough to fill the blender
1 T honey
handful of nuts of choice, chopped

Grandma's Breakfast Smoothie

Place all ingredients except nuts in the blender. Fill blender to 2 inches from the top with water and blend until smooth.

Sprinkle a few chopped nuts on top of each serving.

Variations:
Use peaches instead of apples and pineapple juice in place of orange juice; no need to add water.

Use strawberries instead of apples. Use half orange and half pineapple juice; add water as necessary.

Use ½ of a fresh pineapple instead of the apples. Add apple juice and a handful of unsweetened coconut.

Note from Cindy
I remember Mom making this every morning before school.

From the home of
Jana Elder

Swedish Pancakes

3 eggs
1 ½ C milk
½ tsp. salt
2 T oil or butter
1 T sugar
¾ C flour
½ tsp. baking powder

Beat into a thin batter. Pour and cook on a buttered griddle or frying pan (like crepes).

Serve sprinkled with powdered sugar and lemon juice.

From the home of
Jan and Owen Richardson

1 C sourdough starter (found on
page 39)
2 C flour
2 C milk
1 tsp. salt
2 tsp. baking soda
2 eggs, beaten
3 T melted butter
2 T sugar

Sourdough Pancakes

About 12 hours before planning to serve pancakes, mix sourdough starter with the flour, salt and milk. Let stand in bowl, covered with cheesecloth, in a warm place.

Just before baking the pancakes, remove 1 C of the batter to replenish the starter.

To the remaining batter in the bowl, add baking soda, eggs, melted butter and sugar. Mix well. Bake on a lightly greased hot griddle.

For thinner pancakes add more milk.

From the home of
Jana Elder

German Pancakes

3 eggs
1 ½ C milk
¼ tsp. salt
¼ C butter
⅓ C sugar
¾ C flour

Melt butter in pie plate at 400°.

Mix all ingredients and pour into melted butter in pie plate.

Spoon apple pie filling or spiced apple slices on top to make it extra good.

Bake at 450° for 20 minutes, reduce heat to 350° and bake another 8-10 minutes.

_____

Note from Jana
Another serving suggestion: Spoon Egg Butter on top,
recipe found on next page.

_____

Egg Butter

1 pint water
1 C sugar
½ C water
½ C flour
3 - 4 eggs
½ tsp. vanilla
Dash of salt
½ tsp. Cinnamon
½ tsp. Allspice

In a blender add ½ C water, flour and eggs. Blend until incorporated.

Boil remaining water and sugar together, then pour in the flour and egg mixture and cook until thick and boiling.

Add vanilla, salt, cinnamon and allspice and stir well.

Serve over pancakes.

From the home of
Stuart and Cindy Elder

2 C old fashioned rolled oats
2 C unsweetened almond milk
1- 2 T monk fruit sweetener
¼ tsp. salt
½ tsp. vanilla extract

Topping Options:

[Option 1] 1 T cacao powder
1 T mini chocolate chips

[Option 2] 4 T pumpkin puree
1 tsp. pumpkin pie spice

[Option 3] ½ ripe banana
½ C fresh raspberries

[Option 4] ⅓ apple, diced small
1 tsp. cinnamon

Overnight Oats

In a container with a lid, add first 5 ingredients.

Stir to combine thoroughly. Place a lid on the container and refrigerate overnight.

In the morning, open the container and give it a little stir, then microwave to desired temperature as many servings as desired. They are just as tasty eaten cold.

Add a topping option and enjoy.

Makes 4 servings ½ cup each.

*Oats provide a wide range of health benefits. They help
your digestive system as well as reduce the risk of diabetes and
heart disease. They are high in antioxidants and can
help lower blood sugar, blood pressure and cholesterol levels.*

BREAD, ROLLS, & BISCUITS,

Banana Bread

1 ½ C sugar
¾ C butter, softened
2 eggs
1 tsp. baking soda
½ C buttermilk
¼ tsp. salt
2 C flour
3 ripe bananas, mashed
1 tsp. vanilla

Preheat oven to 300°.

Cream together sugar, butter and eggs.

In a separate container, dissolve baking soda in buttermilk, then add flour and salt.

Combine the buttermilk mixture to the sugar/butter mixture, beating well.

Add the mashed bananas and vanilla. Mix.

Pour into 2 greased loaf pans and bake for 1 hour and 5 minutes.

Notes: ½ C milk and ½ T lemon juice can be substituted for buttermilk.

From the home of
Sarah Elder Lewis

GMA Johnson's Banana Bread

1 C granulated sugar
½ C butter
2 eggs
1 tsp. vanilla
3 ripe bananas
2 C flour
½ tsp. salt
1 tsp. soda
1 C walnuts (optional)

Preheat oven to 350°.

Cream butter and sugar thoroughly. Add vanilla and eggs. Add mashed bananas.

Stir in the dry ingredients, blending until moist. Add nuts if desired.

Bake in two 3 ½ x 7 inch pans or regular loaf pans for 45 minutes or a little longer if needed. Test with a toothpick.

Cranberry Bread

2 C flour
1 C sugar
1 ½ tsp. baking powder
1 tsp. salt
½ tsp. baking soda
1 orange (or 1 T frozen orange)
rind of 1 orange grated
2 T salad oil
1 egg, well beaten
1 C sliced cranberries
½ C chopped nuts

Preheat oven to 350°.

Sift all dry ingredients together.

Put juice of orange in measuring cup. Add 2 T oil and enough water to make ¾ cup. Add to dry ingredients. Add well beaten egg and mix well. Add orange rind, cranberries and nuts.

Bake in greased loaf pan for 1 hour.

Makes 1 loaf.

Note from Dorothy
This is a holiday favorite, but can be enjoyed year round by using frozen cranberries. Frozen cranberries slice well in a salad master. Nuts can be done at the same time. 1 pkg. of cranberries will make 4 loaves. This bread freezes well too.

From the home of
Anne and Rick Roberts

Corn Bread

2 C pancake mix
¾ C sugar
1 C corn meal
2 eggs
1 C milk
¾ C butter
¼ tsp. baking soda

Honey butter
½ C butter
½ C honey

Preheat oven to 350°.

Mix all ingredients in a large bowl and pour into a greased 9 x 13 pan. Bake for 30 minutes.

Make honey butter by melting the butter and then mixing with the honey.

When the corn bread is done cooking, poke holes in it with a fork and drizzle melted honey butter over it.

Enjoy!

From the home of
Eliza and Walter Griffin

1 egg, well beaten
1 C molasses
½ C sugar
½ C lard
1 tsp. baking soda
pinch of salt
dash of all spice
2 C flour

Hot Water Gingerbread

Combine all ingredients then stir in 1 C hot water.

Bake in hot oven.

Note from Cindy
One of the recipes I got from Aunt Marge. There are no more
instructions, so good luck with this one. According to
Aunt Marge, this recipe is taken from the Comforts
Family Guide Cookbook that Eliza used often.

1 ½ active dry yeast
½ C lukewarm water
2 C flour
½ tsp. sugar
½ tsp. salt
2 T olive oil
1 egg, beaten

Italian Pizza Dough

Preheat oven to 400°.

Stir the dry yeast and sugar in the lukewarm water and let stand until a creamy layer forms on top–about 10 minutes.

Mix flour and salt in a large bowl. Mix in olive oil and stir for 2 minutes. Pour yeast mixture and beaten egg into flour mixture and stir to make a stiff dough.

Turn dough out onto a floured surface and knead until springy and smooth. About 8 minutes.

Place dough in an oiled bowl and cover with oiled plastic wrap.

Let dough rise until doubled (about an hour). Punch down and roll out to desired shape.

From the home of
Sarah Elder Lewis

Tortillas

7 C flour
1 yeast envelope (¾ oz.)
salt, big palm full
wheat flour, big fist
sugar, small palm full
1 tsp. baking soda
lard (small pkg.), use ¹/3 of pkg.

Mix dry ingredients well. Add lard cut into small pieces to dry ingredients. Work by hand until flour is a crumbled texture.

Add lukewarm water – approximately 1 ½ cups. Add water slowly making flour ball and continue until one big ball of dough. Knead and knead until soft dough. Check with finger. If dough springs back easily, it should be ready to form small balls. Place balls on cookie sheet and cover with a kitchen towel.

Start rolling out dough by the first row of balls formed. Roll as thick or thin as you like. Cook on flat tortilla grill on medium to hot heat one side at a time. Place warm tortillas in covered towel and cool.

Makes approximately 24 - 30 depending on thickness.

One of Sarah's favorites from her Grandma Ofelia.

From the home of
Jan and Owen Richardson

Snowflake Biscuits

1 pkg. dry yeast
½ C warm water
5 C flour
3 T sugar
1 T baking powder
1 tsp. baking soda
1 tsp salt
¾ C plus 2 T shortening
2 C buttermilk

Preheat oven to 400°.

Dissolve yeast in warm water. Let stand for 10 minutes.

Stir flour, sugar, baking powder, baking soda and salt into a large bowl. Cut in the shortening. Stir in the buttermilk and dissolved yeast. Work only until well moistened.

Put in large covered plastic container and refrigerate to use as needed. This recipe can be kept one week in the refrigerator and used as needed.

Take out only as much as is needed. Carefully roll on a well floured surface ½ to ¾ inch thick. Cut with a 2 ½ inch biscuit cutter.

Bake for 15 minutes. Makes 4 dozen rolls.

Note from Jan
The yeast makes these biscuits taste like rolls. Biscuits can be rolled out, cut and placed on a cookie sheet and frozen. When ready to use, take out what you need and allow 30 minutes at room temperature to thaw, then bake.

From the home of
Kacey and Matty Kahler

Biscuits

1 pkg. dry yeast
½ C warm water
5 C flour
3 T sugar
1 T baking powder
1 tsp. baking soda
1 tsp. salt
¾ C plus 2 T shortening or coconut oil
2 C buttermilk

Preheat oven to 400°.

Dissolve the dry yeast in the warm water and let stand 10 minutes.

To a large bowl add the dry ingredients then cut in the shortening with a pastry cutter. Stir in the yeast/water and buttermilk. Work together until moistened.

Can be stored at this point up to one week in the refrigerator to bake fresh when needed.

Roll out the dough ½ inch to ¾ inch thick. Cut with a 2 ½ inch biscuit cutter. Place on a baking sheet and bake for 15 minutes.

Note from Kacey
Once cut into biscuits, it can be frozen for use at
a later time. This recipe make about 4 dozen.

Onion Garlic Biscuits

1 T oil
1 med. onion chopped
2 garlic cloves, chopped fine
2 cups biscuit mix
½ tsp. dried thyme
²/₃ cup 2% milk

Preheat oven to 450°.

Mix all ingredients only until combined. Too much mixing makes them tough.

Bake for 20 minutes.

Note from Jana
Ponder this: When you agree with a lie you empower a liar.
You have the power over your life to do well or do evil.
Evil never wins.

1 (17 oz.) can family style corn,
1 egg
2 ⅓ C biscuit mix
salad oil

Corn Fritters

Heat 2 - 3 inches of oil in skillet (375°).

Pour liquid from corn into a medium bowl. Add egg and biscuit mix.
Stir until smooth. Fold in the corn.

Drop by tablespoon into the oil. Fry to golden brown, turning once.
Drain on paper towel.

Serve hot or warm. Makes about 3 dozen.

Options: Serve with syrup or gravy or cheese sauce.

Note from Marge
I have done all three options and love the fritters
for variety from potatoes or for breakfast.

Dinner Rolls

2 T dry yeast
2 C warm water
⅓ C sugar
⅓ C shortening, butter or margarine
2 ½ tsp. salt
⅔ C nonfat dry milk
1 egg
5 - 6 C flour

Variation
1 potato boiled and mashed added with the water

Preheat oven to 400°.

Put yeast in water and let stand 5 minutes. Mix in sugar, shortening, salt dry milk, 2 C flour and egg. Beat until smooth. Add flour a little bit at a time until all mixed.

Grease dough and return to bowl. Place in warm place. Let rise until triple in size. Place back on board and let rest 10 minutes, then shape into rolls.

Place rolls on baking sheet. Brush with butter and let rise about 1 ½ hours.

Bake for 15 - 20 minutes.

Makes about 3 dozen rolls.

From the home of
Jan and Owen Richardson

Sourdough Bread

1 pkg. dry yeast
2 T sugar
2 tsp. salt
1 ½ C sourdough starter batter,
recipe on page 39
4 C flour
1 egg

Preheat oven to 350°.

Mix starter, yeast and 1 C warm water. Let stand until yeast is dissolved.

Add remaining ingredients, except egg, mixing well. Knead 10 minutes. Cover and let rise until doubled,. Punch down.

Form into loaves. Cover and let rise until again doubled.

Beat egg and brush over the top before baking.

Bake for 35 - 40 minutes.

From the home of
Kacey and Matty Kahler

Wonton Wrappers

Wrappers
1 egg, beaten
⅓ C water
2 C flour
½ tsp. salt

Mix egg and water in a small bowl. Mix flour and salt in a small bowl. Add flour mixture to the egg mixture to make a dough.

Add 1 tsp. of water if dough is too dry.

Kneed into pliable, elastic dough. Divide in half, roll into 2 balls and cover with a damp cloth for 10 minutes.

Cut the balls into 4 pieces. Roll out each piece to a 10 ½ inch square. Cut each square into 9 - 3 ½ inch squares.

Fill them with anything you want.

From the home of
Jan and Owen Richardson

Sourdough Muffins

1 ½ C whole wheat flour
½ C sugar
1 tsp. salt
1 tsp. baking soda
½ C oil
2 eggs
1 C sourdough starter batter,
recipe on page 39

Preheat oven to 375°.

Combine flour, sugar, salt and baking soda. Stir in oil, eggs and starter batter. Mix only until dry ingredients are moistened.

Bake in greased muffin tins for 30 - 35 minutes or until done.

Makes about 12 muffins.

From the home of
Jan and Owen Richardson

Starter
2 C flour
2 C warm water (90° F)
1 pkg. active dry yeast
1 T sugar

Replenish starter
2 C flour
2 C warm water (90° F)
1 tsp. sugar

Sourdough Starter

Combine all ingredients in a large glass or pottery bowl.

Mix well with a wooden spoon or rubber scraper. It will be lumpy, but it should be.

Cover loosely with wax paper or plastic wrap and let stand in a warm place for 48 hours.

The mixture should be bubbly and have a sour aroma. This makes about 2 ¾ C of sourdough starter.

This is the mixture you will use on all of the recipes. You must replace what you take from it or you will run out of starter.

To replenish the starter add the replenish ingredients to what you have left. Let stand in a warm place for 24 hours or until bubbly and sour.

JAMS, SAUCES & DRESSINGS

From the home of
Jana Elder

2 ½ C green tomatoes, finely
chopped or ground
2 C sugar
1 small box of Jello, any flavor

Green Tomato Jam

In a heavy bottomed sauce pan, add tomatoes and sugar. Stir several times at first, then vigorously as it comes to a full boil.

Boil about 10 minutes. Remove from heat and skim off the foam. Stir in 1 small box of any flavor Jello until it is fully dissolved.

Quickly ladle into prepared jars or freezer containers or bags. Can, freeze or refrigerate.

Note from Jana
Raspberry is my favorite and you cannot tell there are green tomatoes in it. Tomatoes can be ground by using a food processor.

Orange Marmalade

10 oranges
2 lemons
water
sugar

Wash the fruit. Cut in quarters. Cut in very thin slices. Save the juice and the rinds. Discard the pulp or membrane. Cover in heavy kettle with cold water and let stand overnight.

Cook in the same water until peel is tender. Let stand 5 or 6 hours.

Add equal part of sugar. Cook until it is ready to gel. Stir frequently. Pour in hot sterilized jars and seal at once.

Note from Jan
I added some orange Jello for added flavor and to
help it gel. It worked well.

From the home of
Kacey and Matthew Kahler

½ C butter
¾ C lime juice
1 C sugar
2 large eggs
3 large egg yolks
1 T lime zest

Easy Lime Curd

Begin by zesting the limes until you have about 1 T of zest. Be careful to only zest the bright green part of the lime. Set aside

Juice enough limes until you have ¾ C of juice

In a medium bowl, whisk the eggs and egg yolks until smooth. Set aside.

In a medium pan add butter, sugar and lime juice. Heat on medium low just until the butter is melted and the sugar is dissolved.

Pour the warm lime mixture in a slow, steady stream into the eggs, whisking continually until the eggs and the mixture are fully combined. Return the combined mixture to the pan..

Heat the mixture over medium low heat, stirring continually until the mixture has thickened and coats the back of the spoon, approximately 10-15 minutes or until a candy thermometer inserted reaches between 160° and 170°. Do not let the mixture boil.

Remove pan from heat and stir in the lime zest. Pour into heat safe jars. Refrigerate overnight or until fully cooled and set.

From the home of
Jan and Owen Richardson

Raspberry Freezer Jam

4 C raspberries
1 large pkg. Jello (8 serving size)
2 - 3 C sugar

Mix. Put on low heat until Jello and sugar are dissolved.

Bottle and seal.

Cool in refrigerator 24 hours then freeze.

From the home of
Kacey and Matty Kahler

½ C butter/margarine/coconut
oil, in any ratio
pinch of salt
¾ tsp. vanilla
2 ½ C confectioners sugar
⅛ C milk

Butter Cream Frosting

Place all ingredients in a bowl and mix until combined.

This is for a small batch. Recipe can be doubled for a full batch.

2 C chocolate chips
¼ C coconut oil

Magic Shell Recipe

Place all ingredients in a double broiler to melt or 30 second intervals in the microwave.

Pour over freezer treats.

Can keep in a mason jar and reheat for 15 seconds.

Note from Kacey
For Matty's favorite, use white chocolate chips and add
a few drops of cherry flavor and red food coloring.
Pour over vanilla ice cream.

From the home of
Stuart and Cindy Elder

Honey Mustard Dressing

4 T unseasoned rice vinegar
4 T olive oil
½ C plain fat free Greek yogurt
4 T honey mustard
pinch of salt
1 tsp. onion powder
½ tsp. garlic powder
¼ tsp. white pepper
3 - 4 T monk fruit sweetener
1 banana, optional

Place all ingredients in a blender and blend until incorporated.

Note from Cindy
I like my salad dressing on the thick side, so I added the banana one day and was surprised at how good it was. You can't really taste it and it makes the dressing thick and rich.

Jana's Salsa

4 fresh ripe tomatoes
½ small onion
1 mild jalapeno pepper
1/2 tsp. cumin
½ tsp. basil
½ tsp. salt
dash black pepper

Puree all in a blender or food processor, or just chop everything finely and mix. Makes 2 cups.

For a milder version, use just a few chives or a scallion instead of the onion. You may replace the jalapeno pepper with ¼ green pepper.

Note from Jana
Ponder this: Jesus builds his family, his church, not choosing the very best materials as a builder might choose. Jesus chooses for his building the twisted, the rotten, the bruised and the broken. That's you and me. He sees beyond our faults and He sees our potential and our needs. Even if we are messed up with nothing to offer but weakness, rebellious, rejected and with no self-confidence. He has a place for us and makes us beautiful and powerful. We just have to let Him wash us in his blood, bury us in His baptism and He changes our nature.
"God chose the foolish things…to shame the wise…the weak things…to shame the strong…the lowly and despised things…so no one may boast before Him." 1 Cor. 1:27-28

From the home of
Kacey and Matthew Kahler

1 can pineapple chunks
1 can pineapple juice
½ C light brown sugar
¼ C white balsamic vinegar
⅛ C ketchup
2 T soy sauce
3 drops red food coloring
1 T cornstarch

Sweet and Sour Sauce

Combine all ingredients in a sauce pan and bring to a boil over medium heat. Simmer until pineapple is soft and cooked through. Remove pineapple chunks and set aside.

Add 1 T cornstarch with 2 T water and mix thoroughly with fingers until lumps are gone. Add slowly to the sauce and simmer until the sauce thickens. Add food coloring if desired.

Remove from heat and add to food right before serving.

9 large tomatoes
2 ½ T basil
2 T oregano
1 T parsley
1 tsp. ginger
½ tsp. cardamom
¼ tsp. sage
1 tsp. allspice
1 tsp. salt (or more to taste)
1 T sugar
1 T miso
1 T vinegar
1 tsp. sesame oil
stems from 7 mushrooms, diced

Marinara Sauce

Cut out the stems of the tomatoes and cut an X in the bottom of each. Put stem side down in a large pot on low heat. Squeeze out juices as they heat up. Save juice for use in soups later. Once peeling begins, you can easily pull off peels. Mash up tomatoes and strain. Blend tomatoes until pulverized.

In a separate pan, over medium heat add oil. Lightly sauté mushroom stems for one minute, then add all the spices. Add in the blended tomatoes.

Stir miso, salt, sugar and vinegar in a separate bowl with about ½ C of the sauce and mix well. Add to the sauce pan and simmer until desired thickness.

Cardamom has antioxident and diuretic properties and may lower blood pressure. It has anti-inflammatory benefits. It may help with digestive problems including ulcers. Can be used to treat bad breath and prevent cavities.

From the home of
Jana Elder

1T chopped fresh parsley
1 T fresh basil
1 T fresh sage
1 large tomato, chopped
1 clove garlic, finely chopped
salt and pepper to taste
2 T olive oil or grapeseed oil

Uncooked Pasta Sauce

In a bowl, mix together all the herbs and spices, then set aside .

Heat 2 T olive oil or grapeseed oil in a saucepan.

Remove the pan from the heat and add the herbs to the hot oil in the pan to seer, then add the tomatoes.

Pour over precooked pasta and serve topped with grated Parmesan cheese.

2 lb. Velveeta cheese
2 small cans diced green chili peppers
3 tomatoes, peeled and chopped
1 onion, chopped
dash of garlic salt

Chili Con Queso

Place all ingredients in top of a double broiler and simmer for 3 hours, stirring occasionally.

From the home of
Kacey and Matty Kahler

Japanese Style Teriyaki Sauce

2 T gluten free tamari sauce
2 T Marin
3 T Saki
1 T sugar

Place all ingredients in a pan over medium heat and bring to a boil. Reduce heat and simmer until desired consistency.

From the home of
Jan and Owen Richardson

Spaghetti Red Sauce
Low Calorie

¼ C fat free chicken broth
1 small onion
3 T celery leaves
2 C peeled tomatoes (14 ½ oz.
can)
1 C tomato sauce
2 cloves garlic
¼ C dried parsley
1 tsp. Italian seasoning
oregano
bay leaf
¾ tsp. fennel seed

Sauté onion. Combine all ingredients. Simmer together.

Pour over pasta.

From the home of
Kacey and Matty Kahler

Kacey's Taco Seasoning

1 T chili powder
¼ tsp. garlic powder
¼ tsp. onion powder
¼ tsp. crushed red peppers
¼ tsp. oregano
½ tsp. paprika
1 ½ tsp. ground cumin
1 tsp. salt
1 tsp. black or white pepper

Mix all spices together and add to meat while cooking.

CHILI & SOUP

From the home of
Jan and Owen Richardson

Chicken Noodle Soup

2 - 3 carrots, chopped
1 large onion, chopped
2 celery ribs, chopped
handful of mushrooms, chopped
2 - 3 hands full of noodles
salt
white pepper
onion powder
garlic powder
chicken bouillon

Boil pieces of chicken in a gallon of water. When tender, remove chicken and set aside.

Add the vegetables to the water. As the vegetables are cooking, add the noodles. Cook until vegetables are tender.

Remove chicken from bones and chop. Add to the soup. Season with salt, white pepper, onion and garlic powder to taste.

This was one of the recipes Jan served at the cafeteria when she worked as head chef for UVCC.

1 can chili with beans and meat
1 can whole kernel corn with liquid
1 can (14 oz.) diced tomatoes with liquid
1 can (8 oz.) tomato sauce
1 can (15 oz.) black beans with liquid
1 ½ - 3 T dry taco seasoning mix

Easy Taco Soup

Combine all ingredients in a greased 4 quart or larger slow cooker.

Cover and cook on low for 6-8 hours.

4 - 6 servings.

From the home of
Sarah Elder Lewis

3 C dry black beans
1 ¾ lbs. spicy sausages
1 T olive oil
4 cloves garlic, finely chopped
2 yellow onions, finely chopped
2 celery stalks, finely chopped
2 ½ qt. chicken stock
4 T fresh parsley, finely chopped
1 tsp. dried oregano
½ tsp. ground cumin
2 bay leaves
½ T salt
½ C sour cream
2 T fresh chives, finely chopped
2 T fresh cilantro, finely chopped

In loving memory of Sarah's Dad,
Jon. One of his favorite meals.

Sausage and Black Bean Soup

Sort through the beans, discarding any impurities or discolored ones. Set aside. Remove the casings from 1 pound of the sausages. In a large sauté pan warm the oil over medium heat and add the sausages. Coarsely break up the sausages with a wooden spoon and sauté for about 5 minutes.

Pour off all but about 3 T of the fat and add garlic, onions and celery and sauté until the onions are translucent or about 2-3 minutes. Add the beans, stock, parsley, oregano, cumin and bay leaves and bring to a boil. Reduce the heat, cover and simmer until beans are very tender, about 2 ½ hours. Add half of the salt halfway through the cooking and add a little water if necessary to keep the beans moist.

Discard the bay leaves. Pour a few ladlefuls of beans into a food processor or blender and puree. Stir back into the pan with the remaining salt. Season to taste. Cut the remaining sausages into slices ½" thick. Sauté in a nonstick frying pan over medium heat until browned. Ladle soup into bowls and garnish with sour cream, sausage slices, chives and cilantro.

Serves 6 - 8.

From the home of
Jan and Owen Richardson

Mushroom Soup

1 ½ lbs. mushrooms, sliced
1 large onion, diced
¾ gallon water
1 ½ C coffee creamer
1 T beef bouillon
corn starch
salt, white pepper, onion powder
and garlic powder to taste

Slice and fry mushrooms and onions in butter. Add water, creamer and bouillon.

Thicken with corn starch and season to taste.

*This was one of the recipes Jan served at the cafeteria
when she worked as head chef for UVCC.*

From the home of
Kacey and Matthew Kahler

1 ½ T butter
2 large leeks, roughly chopped
1 ½ cloves garlic, finely chopped
1 pound Yukon gold potatoes,
roughly chopped
3 ½ C chicken broth
1 bay leaf
1 - 2 sprigs fresh thyme
½ tsp. salt
¼ tsp. pepper
½ C heavy cream
chives, finely chopped

Potato Leek Soup

Melt the butter in a large soup pot over medium heat. Add the leeks and garlic. Stir until leeks are soft and wilted or about 10 minutes.

Add the chicken broth, potatoes, bay leaf, thyme, salt and pepper to the pot and bring it to a boil. Cover and reduce the heat to low. Simmer for 15 minutes or until potatoes are soft.

Remove the thyme sprigs and bay leaf, then puree the soup until smooth. Add in the heavy cream and bring to a simmer. Soup will thicken the longer you simmer it. If it is too thick, add more broth to thin it out.

Serve topped with fresh chives.

Leeks are rich in antioxidants and may have anti-inflammatory and anti-diabetic properties. They contain a compound called allicin that may protect the body from cellular damage. High in vitamin A, which supports eye health, skin health, cardiovascular health and help with respiratory problems such as flu, cold and cough.

1 large can V-8 juice
dash of Italian seasoning
cooked spaghetti, broken in pieces

Optional:
minced onion
hamburger, browned and drained

Spaghetti Soup

Heat 1 large can of V-8 juice.   Add a dash of Italian seasoning.
Simmer 5 minutes. Add cooked spaghetti and heat through.

Note from Marge
*I often add minced onion to this for a change and even a little
hamburger, browned and drained. This was made at the Holendease
Restaurant in the # 1 Wilshire building in Los Angeles, where I
worked for Mr. Man.*

From the home of
Jan and Owen Richardson

Gazpacho

1 clove garlic
4 ripe tomatoes, peeled and quartered
½ small onion
1 cucumber, peeled and sliced
1 tsp. salt
¼ tsp. white pepper
2 T olive oil
2 T vinegar
½ C water

Fill blender container with vegetables. Add seasonings, olive oil, vinegar and water. Use about half the ingredients at one time.

Cover and blend for just 2 seconds. Chill in refrigerator or pour into soup plates and serve with an ice cube in the center of each serving.

This was one of the recipes Jan served at the cafeteria when she worked as head chef for UVCC.

1- 2 cans chicken breast, drained
1 large can vegetarian baked beans
2 cans diced fire roasted tomatoes
1 can corn, drained
1 can black beans, drained and rinsed
1 can kidney beans, drained and rinsed
1 pkg. taco seasoning mix
sour cream, optional
scallions, optional

Chicken Taco Chili

Prepare the beans as directed and place in a pot on the stove over medium-high heat or in a crock pot.   Add in the fire roasted tomatoes and stir to combine..

Add the chicken breast and the taco seasonings. Bring to a boil and reduce the heat to low and simmer for an hour or more.

Serve topped with sour cream and scallions if desired.

Makes 6 servings.

Note from Cindy
This is a great recipe for those who are watching their weight.
It is only 2 weight watchers points per serving.

From the home of
Jan and Owen Richardson

Clam Chowder

3 potatoes, diced
2 carrots, diced
2 large onions, diced
2 celery ribs, diced
1 - 2 cans clams, juice and all
1 ½ - 2 C coffee creamer powder
cornstarch to thicken
salt
white pepper
onion powder
½ tsp. Worcestershire sauce

In 4 quarts of water, boil the vegetables. When they are mostly soft, add in the clams and creamer.

Thicken with corn starch and season with onion powder, salt and white pepper to taste. Add ½ tsp Worcestershire sauce.

This was one of the recipes Jan served at the cafeteria when she worked as head chef for UVCC.

From the home of
Stuart and Cindy Elder

Potato Corn Chowder

5 C water
4-5 medium size Yukon gold
potatoes, cubed
1 medium size onion, chopped (I
use Vidalia sweet onions)
1 can corn, drained (16 oz.)
½ C powdered non-dairy creamer
1 T onion powder
¼ C butter
1 tsp. basil
1 T salt (or to taste)
pepper to taste
3 T corn starch

In a large pan place the water on high heat.

Peel potatoes, cut into cubes and place in the water. Next add the chopped onion and continue to boil for 5 minutes or until the potatoes are tender. Turn down the heat and add the creamer and all the spices.

In a small bowl add the corn starch and 3 - 4 T water. Mix with your fingers to make sure all the lumps are gone and then pour slowly into the soup, stirring until you have reached the level of thickness that you like your soup.

Add the corn and butter and stir until butter is melted. Serve topped with shredded cheese (optional).

SANDWICHES & SALADS

From the home of
Kacey and Matthew Kahler

10 oz. spaghetti
1 red bell pepper, thinly sliced
2 large carrots, peeled and grated
1 C green onions, finely chopped
1 C cilantro, finely chopped
2 C grated cabbage, or finely chopped

Dressing
1 T minced ginger
2 cloves garlic, minced (optional)
½ C peanut butter
1 ½ T rice vinegar
¼ C soy sauce
2 T lime juice
2 ½ T maple syrup
½ tsp. red pepper flakes or 1 T Sriracha sauce (for spicy sauce
2 - 4 T water to adjust consistency

Topping Suggestions
peanuts or cashews
squeeze of lime juice
fresh cilantro or Thai basil
Sriracha

Cold Asian Noodle Salad

Bring a pot of water to a boil and cook pasta according to package instructions.

Chop all the vegetables while the pasta is cooking and place them in a large bowl.

Make the dressing by blending all the ingredients until smooth and creamy. To adjust the consistency, add water a tablespoon at a time. Dressing should be thick and creamy but still pourable.

When the pasta is done cooking, drain and rinse under cold water, then add the pasta to the bowl with the chopped vegetables.

Top with sauce and mix well.

Serve right away, topped with desired toppings.

Leftovers can be stored in the refrigerator for up to 4 days.

From the home of
Stuart and Cindy Elder

2 ½ C boneless, skinless chicken
breast, cooked
1 C fresh blueberries
⅓ C sliced almonds
½ C celery, finely chopped
¼ C Vidalia onion, finely chopped

Honey Mustard Dressing
found on page 47

Blueberry Almond Chicken Salad

Layer all ingredients over shredded cabbage and serve with honey mustard dressing.

OR mix all ingredients together with honey mustard dressing and serve on toast.

Blueberries are low in calories and high in nutrients.
They may help lower blood pressure and prevent heart disease.
They are known as the king of antioxidant foods.

Waldorf Salad

4 -5 apples, diced
2 celery ribs, diced
½ C walnuts, chopped
mayonnaise
honey
cinnamon

Leave the peelings on the apples. Core and dice them. Place in a large bowl. Dice the celery and chop the walnuts. Add to the apples.

Add a spoonful of mayonnaise and stir. Add another spoonful until everything is well coated.

Stir in a spoonful of honey. Taste and add more to reach the desired sweetness.

Sprinkle in some cinnamon. Taste and sprinkle in more if desired,

Note from Cindy
Mom didn't use recipes but she knew how to make
things tasty. This was one of my favorites.

From the home of
Jan and Owen Richardson

Cranberry Jello Salad

1 small box raspberry Jello
1 C hot water
dash of salt
½ C cold water
2 tsp. lemon juice
1 C whole cranberry sauce
½ C diced celery
½ C pineapple, drained

Mix Jello and hot water. When dissolved add salt, cold water and lemon juice.

Partially set in fridge. Then fold in cranberry, celery and pineapple.

Return to fridge and set until firm.

From the home of
Stuart and Cindy Elder

1 large box raspberry Jello
1 small box strawberry Jello
3 C boiling water
1 can crushed pineapple (20 oz.)
8 oz. bag fresh cranberries
1 ¼ C pecans, chopped

Topping
12 oz. cream cheese, softened
⅓ C sour cream
1 tsp. vanilla
1 C powdered sugar

Fresh Cranberry Jello Salad

Pour the Jello packages into a 9 x 11 glass dish and add the boiling water. Stir until completely dissolved.

Add cold water, crushed pineapple with juice, chopped cranberries and 1 cup chopped pecans. Stir to combine.

Place in refrigerator to set for at least 4 hours.

To make topping, combine all ingredients in a medium size bowl and mix with a hand mixer until smooth.

Spread evenly over the firm Jello. Top with a sprinkling of chopped pecans.

From the home of
Owen and Janet Richardson

Fruity Pistachio Salad

1 small box pistachio pudding mix
1 can pineapple tidbits (16 oz.)
1 can crushed pineapple (8 oz.)
1 C shredded coconut
1 C pecans, chopped
1 container of whipped topping
1 C miniature marshmallows

Mix both cans of pineapple with the juice and sprinkle the pudding mix on the top of it. Let it sit for about 3 minutes.

Carefully mix in the nuts and the coconut. Slowly fold in the whipped topping and the marshmallows.

Refrigerate for at least 2 hours before serving.

From the home of
Jan and Owen Richardson

1 can pineapple chunks (20 oz.)
1 can fruit cocktail, drained
1 can mandarin oranges, drained
3 bananas, sliced
1 pkg. instant lemon pudding,
(3 oz.)

Fruit Salad

Combine fruit in a large bowl. Sprinkle pudding into the fruit and mix well.

Chill.

Sloppy Salad

2 -3 garden ripe tomatoes
1 cucumber
1 avocado
mayonnaise
salt
pepper

Cut tomatoes, cucumbers and avocado into bite size pieces. Place in a large bowl. Stir in a fair amount of mayonnaise.

Add salt and pepper to taste.

Note from Cindy
When she had it, Mom would add some vegetable
broth powder. This is good to eat as a salad but
is also good on toast.

From the home of
Scott and Anita Griffin

Scott's Favorite Salad

3 large garden ripe tomatoes
2 cucumbers
1 mandarin orange
3 T olive oil
1 - 2 T rice vinegar
1 - 2 tsp. honey
fresh basil, chopped
salt to taste
pepper to taste

Cut tomatoes and cucumbers into bite size pieces. Place in a large bowl.

Add only the juice of the mandarin orange.

Add the rest of the ingredients to the bowl and stir to combine.

From the home of
Jana Elder

Tortellini Picnic Salad

1 pkg. tortellini (12 oz.)
2 - 3 jars artichoke hearts (6 oz.)
marinated in oil, drained and
quartered
2 - 2 ½ C tomatoes, diced
1 C feta cheese, crumbled
1 - 2 cans sliced black olives,
drained
1 C walnuts, chopped
½ C green onions, chopped

Dressing
½ C wine vinegar
6 cloves garlic, minced
2 T dried basil
2 tsp. dried dill

Make dressing a day ahead and refrigerate (if you remember).

Cook, drain and chill the tortellini.

When chilled, add the rest of the ingredients.

Toss with the dressing.

Note from Jana
Absolutely delicious, a show stopper. I love this pull out of the cooler
and eat salad. Ponder this: If you think God is your enemy, you'll
have no one to call to. God is ABSOLUTELY GOOD.

From the home of
Jana Elder

Pesto Zucchini and Corn Quinoa Salad

1 C quinoa, rinsed
1 ¾ C water or broth
1 T olive oil
2 cloves garlic, chopped
4 C zucchini (2 medium), diced
1 C corn, fresh or frozen
salt and pepper to taste
1 (15 oz.) can of chickpeas, rinsed
and drained (or 1 ½ C cooked
beans from ½ C dry)
¼ C green onions, sliced
¼ C pine nuts, toasted
½ C basil pesto
2 T lemon juice

Bring water and quinoa to a boil. Reduce heat and simmer, covered, until quinoa is tender and has absorbed the water, about 15 minutes. Remove from heat and let sit for 5 minutes, covered.

Meanwhile, prep zucchini and corn. Heat oil over med-high heat and add the zucchini and corn. Cook until tender, about 12 minutes.

Before removing from heat, add salt and pepper. Mix everything together and serve.

Note from Jana
Ponder this: My favorite movie, Dances with Wolves, remember the part where he is so distraught that he rides a horse back and forth between the two battle fronts hoping to get shot but doesn't? In this day and age weapons are far more accurate and destructive. Towards the end Lt. John Dunbar is faced with a critical decision to examine his heart and soul before making a heroic choice that determines his destiny. We are at that crossroad today. Get yourself on the right side early or get run over. There is no middle fence. If there was, it would be for target practice.

Fennel Chicken Salad

1 can chicken breast
1 - 2 celery ribs, chopped
¼ C cashews
¼ C mayonnaise
salt, to taste
white pepper, to taste
¼ tsp. fennel seed or fennel root
minced
1 Fuji apple, cubed

Combine all ingredients together except cashews and mix well.

Serve on toast or bread of choice. Also good served on top of a bed of lettuce. Also just good to eat all by itself.

Fennel is a very beneficial herb. It is known to curb appetite, benefit heart health, lower blood pressure, reduce inflammation, has antioxidant, anti-fungal and antiviral effects. Fennel tea may aid digestion and help with heartburn, bloating and colic in infants.

From the home of
Stuart and Cindy Elder

Barbeque Chickpea Salad

1 can chickpeas, drained
½ C barbeque sauce
1 can corn
¼ C onion, finely chopped
2 celery ribs, finely chopped
3 T mayonnaise
lettuce, chopped
avocado, sliced

Place first 6 ingredients in a bowl and stir to combine.

Serve on top of a bed of lettuce and top with a few avocado slices.

From the home of
Dee and Hal Reddick

1 can kidney beans, drained well
1 onion, finely chopped
cheddar cheese, grated
salad dressing

Kidney Bean Salad

Mix all ingredients with salad dressing. Use own judgment on amount of cheese.

Chill and serve.

Notes from Marge
I often add a couple of celery sticks chopped finely to this recipe.

2 C mayonnaise
2 C salad dressing
¼ C vinegar
2 tsp. accent
4 tsp. mustard
1 C sugar
1 green pepper, chopped
1 C celery, chopped
2 dozen eggs, cooked
1 ¼ lbs. salad shrimp
8 C shell macaroni

Shrimp Macaroni Salad

Cook macaroni and drain. Combine other ingredients and mix well with the macaroni.

Chill.

From the home of
Jan and Owen Richardson

¾ C light mayonnaise
½ tsp. ground ginger
½ tsp. salt
½ C chopped walnuts
3 C cooked chicken, chopped
1 ½ C red seedless grapes
1 C celery, sliced
½ C green onions, sliced

New West Chicken Salad

Combine mayonnaise, ginger and salt. Stir in remaining ingredients.
Cover and chill.

Makes 5 ½ cups.

From the home of
Jan and Owen Richardson

Oriental Cabbage Salad

1 cooked chicken breast, chopped
2 T toasted sesame seeds
2 T toasted sliced almonds
1 pkg. uncooked Ramen noodles
½ head cabbage, thinly sliced
2 green onions, chopped with tops

Dressing
2 T sugar
½ C salad oil
1 tsp. salt
1 tsp. accent
½ tsp. pepper
3 T vinegar

Prepare salad dressing.

Mix salad ingredients together in a large bowl and pour the dressing over it. Stir to combine.

Serve chilled. Keeps well.

From the home of
Marge Ault

Rice Salad

1 C cooked rice
green peppers, chopped
green onion, chopped
cucumbers, chopped
radishes, chopped
salad dressing

Mix all ingredients together with a little salad dressing and season to taste. All the Veggies together equal ½ C total.

Variation:
1 can peas and carrots, drained
½ C celery and onion, chopped

Note from Marge
These are a nice change from potato salad.
Sent to me by my best friend Dollie. Chopped cheese
is good added to both of these salads.

Option 1
zucchini, shredded
sprouted bread, toasted
grapeseed mayonnaise
avocado, sliced
curry powder
spike seasoning

Option 2
zucchini, cut up
onions, chopped
tomato sauce (Hunt's basil and
oregano is best)

Zucchini Toast

For option 1:

Shred enough zucchini for the amount of open faced toasted sandwiches you desire. Peel and slice the avocado.

Toast the bread and spread it with desired amout of grapeseed mayonnaise. Top with shredded zucchini and avocado slices.

Sprinkle with curry and spike.

For option 2:

Stir fry the zucchini and onions. Don't overcook them.

Mix in the sauce and serve over toast.

Note from Maureen
*This is the way we eat. We don't use recipes just a little of
this and a little of that! Adrian cooks just about anything in the
instant pot like corn on the cob, baked potatoes and other
vegetables, vegetable soup and vegetable chili.*

From the home of
Ryan Griffin Kent

2 slices of bread (Food for life
Ezekiel 4:9)
creamy whipped honey
banana
cinnamon

Creamy Honey Toast

Toast the bread. Spread with the creamy whipped honey. Top with sliced bananas and sprinkle with cinnamon.

Note: Raw honey is a good source of antioxidants. It has antibacterial and antifungal properties and can be used to heal wounds. It helps with digestion and soothes a sore throat.

Note from Ryan

I remember grandma Griffin always making me toast with honey and banana…maybe cinnamon too? She used whipped honey which I still haven't found that tastes like what she used. I'll never forget it. She was trying to explain the type of honey to me as a kid one time. She said that all you had to do was add a spoonful of this special honey to any honey and it would change to her good honey. I still don't get it but I believe her. Ha ha!

From the home of
Marge Ault

Tomato Toast

2 eggs, slightly beaten
½ tsp. salt
½ C condensed tomato soup
6 slices of bread
cheese sauce

Combine soup, egg and salt. Cut bread slices in half for easy handing. Dip bread slices in the mixture and sauté in hot shortening on griddle until golden brown on both sides.

Serve with a cheese sauce.

Note from Marge
I love french toast so this is a nice change from it.
Great for late evening meal or even lunch if served
with a mixed vegetable salad.

VEGETABLES & SIDE DISHES

From the home of
Jan and Owen Richardson

Baked Bean Medley

2 C onion, chopped
1 C green pepper, chopped
2 cans pork and beans (31 oz.)
1 can kidney beans (15 oz.)
1 can red beans (15 oz.)
1 can lima or great northern beans
½ lb. bacon, cooked, drained and
broken into small pieces
1 ½ C barbeque sauce (Kraft
hickory smoked is good)
½ C brown sugar
3 T vinegar

Preheat oven to 350°.

Cook onions and peppers. Drain all beans except the pork and beans.
Combine all.

Bake for 1 hour.

Serves 24.

From the home of
Marc & Erika Bird

4 lbs. sweet potatoes, peeled and
cut into 1-inch cubes
5 T butter
⅔ C brown sugar
1 tsp. ground cinnamon
¼ tsp. ground nutmeg
½ tsp. salt
pinch of ground ginger

Toppings
2 C mini marshmallows
½ C pecans, chopped

Candied Sweet Potatoes

Preheat oven to 375°.

Place sweet potatoes in a 9x13 glass baking dish. Combine butter, brown sugar and spices in a small saucepan over medium heat. Bring to a boil and stir until sugar dissolves. Pour mixture over sweet potatoes and toss to coat. Cover with foil.

Bake for 50 minutes then uncover and bake until sweet potatoes are tender and syrup thickens a bit. Baste occasionally for about 20 minutes.

Increase oven temperature to 500°. Top the sweet potatoes with marshmallows and pecans. Bake until the marshmallows begin to melt and brown, about 3 minutes.

Note from Marc
I always remember the candied yams being a staple with my family for holiday meals when I was young. Back then it was always canned yams and such. As I work for Whole Foods, I try to cook fresh as much as possible. I cook this every Thanksgiving when I am hosting.

From the home of
Stuart and Cindy Eder

8 - 10 carrots, about 5 cups sliced
2 T honey
1 - 2 tsp. curry powder
½ tsp. salt
3 T butter
1 tsp. soy sauce

Stuart's Curried Carrots

Place about a inch and a half of water in a medium size pan and turn on high and bring to a boil.

Peel and slice the carrots and add them to the boiling water. Boil about 5 minutes or until tender.

Drain and put carrots into a sauté pan or wok on high heat and add butter, then the rest of the ingredients one at a time. Stir between each ingredient.

This recipe makes a good amount for taking to a potluck.

Curry is a blend of spices that has some good health benefits.
It contains antioxidants, and helps with inflammatory issues,
is anti-bacterial and antifungal.

From the home of
Jana Elder

Zucchini Onion Pie

3 eggs
1 C Parmesan Cheese
½ C oil
1 T minced parsley
1 clove garlic
¼ tsp. salt
⅛ tsp. pepper
1 C biscuit mix
1 small onion
3 C sliced zucchini

Preheat oven to 350°.

Mix all ingredients together and place in a greased cake pan or glass baking dish.

Bake for 25 minutes.

Note from Jana
Ponder this: When you agree with a lie you empower a liar.
You have the power over your life to do well or do evil.
Evil never wins.

From the home of
Stuart and Cindy Eder

Stuart's House Rice

½ cube butter
mushrooms, sliced
green peppers, slices
onions, sliced
2 C rice (I use Uncle Ben's)
2 ¼ C Water
1 tsp. seasoning mix (see notes)
2 T soy sauce

Melt butter in a sauce pan, then add vegetables and uncooked rice. Mix until the rice is coated with the butter.

Add water and seasoning mix. Turn heat to high until the water boils, then lower the heat to low. Cover and simmer 20 minutes. Don't lift the lid until the time is up.

Note from Stuart
Seasoning mix is 8 parts salt, 1 part white pepper and 1 part garlic, (a part can be whatever you choose - like a Tablespoon). Mix thoroughly. Make as much you want to make. It is a good mix to have on hand.

Basil Rice

¼ C butter
2 T chopped onion
1 ½ T wine vinegar
½ tsp. salt
½ tsp. sugar
1 tsp. basil
3 C cooked rice

Brown onions in butter over medium heat.

Add remaining ingredients except rice and mix together.

Add cooked rice.

Note from Jana
Ponder this: What is small to you could be huge to
someone else.

From the home of
Stuart and Cindy Eder

5 T olive oil
½ C onion, diced (I use Vidalia
sweet onions)
½ C mushrooms, sliced (optional)
½ C frozen petite peas
2 eggs
3 C cooked white rice (I use
Jasmine rice)
1 C diced black forest ham
3 T soy sauce
1 tsp. sesame oil (optional)
1 tsp. onion powder
salt and pepper to taste

Ham Fried Rice

In a large frying pan or wok turn heat on high. Add 3 T olive oil, onions and mushrooms; sauté until onions are caramelized and mushrooms are browned.

In a small bowl beat the eggs with a fork. Push the vegetables to one side of the pan. Add 2 T olive oil. Pour the eggs into the oil and cook. Use a rubber spatula to scramble the eggs and mix them into the other vegetables.

Turn temperature down to low and add the cooked rice, peas (no need to thaw) and the ham, and stir. Add soy sauce, sesame oil, salt and pepper if desired. Continue over low heat until warm throughout.

Note from Cindy
I use Bragg's Liquid Aminos instead of soy sauce; it is
a perfect alternative and is gluten free. This dish is also good
without the ham for the vegetarian.

From the home of
Jan and Owen Richardson

Hash Brown
Potato Casserole

1 pkg. frozen hash browns (32 oz.)
1 C butter, melted
1 can cream of chicken soup
12 oz. grated American cheese
1 C sour cream (8 oz.)
1 tsp. salt
½ small onion, chopped
2 C crushed cornflakes

Preheat oven to 350°.

Place hash browns in a 9 x 13 inch baking pan.

Mix half the butter with the soup, cheese, sour cream, salt and onion. Pour over potatoes.

Mix the rest of the melted butter with the cornflakes and place on top of casserole.

Bake for 45 minutes.

From the home of
Stuart and Cindy Elder

Stu's Potatoes

10 potatoes, baked
2 large onions, chopped
½ C olive oil
2 tsp. Spike seasoning
¼ tsp. garlic powder
dash of cayenne pepper
dash of salt
¼ C soy sauce

Leaving the skin on, chop the pre-baked potatoes into cubes.

Sauté onions in oil and then add spices. Add in the potatoes and stir to combine with the oil and onion mixture.

When potatoes are warmed through, add in the soy sauce and stir to combine.

Serve topped with scallions or chives if desired.

From the home of
Jan and Owen Richardson

Zucchini Provençale

1 medium onion, sliced
1 clove garlic, minced
¼ C salad oil
4 tomatoes, cut up
1 green pepper, chopped
salt and pepper to taste
parsley
parmesan cheese

In skillet, sauté onion and garlic in oil. Add zucchini, tomatoes, green peppers, salt and pepper.

Cook until tender.

Sprinkle with parsley and parmesan cheese before serving.

Makes 8 servings.

From the home of
Jana Elder

Pasta with Zucchini Tomato Sauce

12 oz. pasta of choice
2 large zucchini coarsely grated
(1 ¾ lbs.)
3 T unsalted butter
2 C cherry tomatoes (halved) or
chopped tomatoes
½ tsp. finely grated lemon zest
pepper and salt
½ C grated Parmesan cheese, plus
more for topping
1 small bunch chives, cut in
1 inch pieces

Toss zucchini with ½ tsp. salt and place in a colander over a bowl for 10 min. Gently squeeze excess moisture from zucchini.

Meanwhile, cook pasta and save out ½ cup cooking water.

Heat butter in a large skillet over medium heat. Add the chopped tomatoes and cook 4 minutes. Add zucchini and lemon zest and cook another 4 minutes. Add salt and pepper.

Transfer into a large bowl. Add pasta and cheese and toss. Add in ¼ cup cooking liquid (or more) and chives. Top and serve.

Note from Jana
Ponder this: No religion is a go-between or middle-man.
It's you and God, period!

MEATS & MAIN DISHES

From the home of
Jan and Owen Richardson

1 ½ C flour
1 ½ tsp. baking powder
½ tsp. baking soda
½ tsp. dill weed
½ tsp. finely shredded lemon peel
8 oz. carton of sour cream
8 slices of bacon
½ C ricotta cheese
½ C shredded Swiss cheese
3 oz. cream cheese
3 T milk
2 tsp. Dijon mustard
1 green onion, finely chopped
1 T snipped parsley

Cheese, Bacon and Bread Bake

Preheat oven to 400°.

In a medium bowl combine flour, baking powder, baking soda, dill weed and lemon peel. Stir in sour cream.

On a floured surface, knead dough till smooth. Cover and set aside.

In a 10" oven safe skillet, cook bacon till crisp. Drain and crumble. Set aside.

Cool skillet and wipe with a paper towel. Press dough onto the bottom and half inch up the sides of the skillet; sprinkle with all but 2 T of the crumbled bacon.

Combine cheeses, milk, mustard, onion and parsley; spread into skillet.

Bake for 25 minutes or until golden. Cool slightly. Sprinkle with reserved bacon and cut into wedges.

Serves 8.

From the home of
Joseph and Lilly Jacoby

2 C cooked chicken, cut into bite
sized pieces
¼ tsp. pepper
½ C cashew nuts
2 C diced celery
½ C minced onion
2 cans chow mein noodles
2 cans cream of mushroom soup

Chicken Casserole

Preheat oven to 325°.

Reserve some of the chow mein noodles for the top. Combine all ingredients and place in a greased casserole dish. Pour 2 cans of diluted mushroom soup over it.

Bake for 45 minutes and top with the remaining noodles for the last 15 minutes.

Note from Cindy
One of the recipes I got from Aunt Marge.

From the home of
Kacey and Matthew Kahler

4 ribs of celery, chopped
1 med. onion, chopped
1 T oil or butter
8 - 10 chicken tenderloins
½ tsp. white pepper
1 tsp. thyme
¾ tsp. salt
6 C water
1 slice bread
10 oz. extra large egg noodles
8 oz. sour cream
2 T flour
½ tsp. garlic
2 T parsley

Chicken Noodle Casserole

Preheat oven to 375°.

In a small bowl, tear the bread into small pieces. Finely chop the remaining celery and onion and toss it with the bread. Set aside.

In a wok, cook two thirds of the celery and onion in hot oil over medium heat for 3 minutes. Add chicken, pepper, thyme and salt. Cook for 2 minutes Add the water and bring it to a boil, then reduce the heat and simmer covered for 20 - 25 minutes until chicken is cooked thoroughly. Remove the chicken to a cutting board to cool slightly. Add noodles to the simmering broth and boil for 7 - 8 minutes.

To make the sauce, whisk together the sour cream, flour and garlic in a medium sized bowl. Gradually add in 1 cup of the hot broth and stir until smooth. Add this mixture to the remaining broth in the pan. Cook stirring continuously until boiling.

Chop the chicken into small pieces and add back to the pot and stir.

Pour into a baking dish and sprinkle with the bread and spices mixture then spray lightly with a cooking spray. Bake uncovered for 30 - 35 minutes or until the topping begins to brown. Garnish with parsley if desired.

From the home of
Stuart and Cindy Eder

1 pkg. cream cheese, softened
(8 oz. block)
1 C shredded cheese (any kind will
do, I use a mixture)
1 pkg. of frozen spinach, thawed
2 cans refrigerated crescent rolls
melted butter
seasoned bread crumbs
1 can cream of mushroom soup
1 C sour cream

Cheesy Spinach Pillows

Preheat oven to 375°.

Squeeze most of the moisture out of the thawed spinach and place in
a bowl. Add cream cheese and mix well. Stir in shredded cheese.

Unroll the crescent dough and press two triangles together, pressing
the seams well to make eight rectangles. Put a good amount of filling
on one half of each crescent rectangle (a little more than ¼ cup). Fold
the top half over and seal the edges, making sure the filling stays
inside.

In a small bowl place the melted butter and in another small bowl
place the bread crumbs. Dip each pillow into the melted butter and
then into the bread crumbs. Place on an ungreased cookie sheet and
bake 15 - 18 minutes or until golden brown.

In a small saucepan place the can of soup and the sour cream. Warm
over low heat. Pour over each pillow when serving.

From the home of
Jan and Owen Richardson

Chili Relleno Casserole

2 cans green chilies, (4 oz.) seeded
and cut into 1 inch strips
1 lb. cheddar cheese
1 lb. Monterey jack cheese
1 can condensed milk
4 - 5 T flour
2 cans tomato sauce (8oz.)
4 eggs
salt and pepper to taste

Preheat oven to 325°.

In a 9 x 13 pan, layer half of the chilies, all of the cheddar, then the second half of the chilies followed by all of the jack cheese.

Separate the eggs and beat the whites until stiff. Mix the egg yolks, flour, salt and pepper with the milk. Fold in the beaten egg whites and pour over the layers.

Bake for 30 minutes.

Remove from oven and pour tomato sauce over the top. Bake another 30 minutes.

From the home of
Marc & Erika Bird

4 lbs. beef chuck roast, cut into 3
inch chunks
1 onion, diced
3 - 4 chipotles in adobo sauce,
finely diced
5 garlic cloves, minced
¼ C fresh lime juice
2 T apple cider vinegar
1 T ground cumin
½ T dried oregano
2 tsp. salt
1 tsp. black pepper
¼ tsp. ground cloves
¾ C beef stock
3 bay leaves
cilantro
lime wedges

Mexican Beef Barbacoa

Add all of the ingredients except the bay leaves, to the bowl of a slow cooker.

Gently toss and mix all together, then add the bay leaves and cover. Cook on low for 8 - 9 hours or on high for 4 - 5 hours. The beef should be tender and fall apart easily.

Remove the beef and shred with a two forks.

Place the shredded beef back in the slow cooker and stir to combine.

Serve the barbacoa straight from the slow cooker. Serve with cilantro and lime wedges.

Note from Marc
We live in San Diego and we eat a lot of tacos. This recipe
has always been a hit when we have friends over.

From the home of
Kacey and Matthew Kahler

4 chicken breasts
salt and pepper to taste
olive oil

Sauce
1 tsp. fresh lime basil
½ tsp. sage
½ tsp. lemon thyme
1 C milk
salt and pepper to taste
1 tsp. corn starch

Creamy Herb Chicken

Season chicken breasts generously with salt and pepper.

Heat 1 T oil in a large skillet over med-high heat. Cook the chicken breasts until done (about 5 minutes each side depending on the thickness). Transfer to a plate and set aside.

In the same skillet, heat 2 tsp olive oil and sauté the herbs for about a minute or until fragrant.

Stir in milk and season with salt and pepper. Bring mixture to a boil. In a small cup add 1 tsp. corn starch with 1 T water and mix with fingers until lumps are gone. Add the cornstarch and stir until sauce has thickened slightly. Reduce heat and simmer for a minute more.

Return chicken to the skillet with the sauce.

Serve immediately.

Spaghetti Stuffed Peppers

4 large green peppers
2 cans spaghetti with meat sauce
(15 ½ oz. each)
1 C cheese cracker crumbs (like
Cheez-its)
¼ C water

Preheat oven to 350°.

Cut peppers in half lengthwise. Remove seeds and membrane.

Allow peppers to stand in boiling water for 10 minutes. Drain well.

Fill halves with spaghetti and top with the crumbs. Arrange in a shallow baking dish. Add water and bake for 25 minutes or until tender.

Note from Marge
This is a good way to fix peppers. I like them served
with cold V-8 juice and garlic bread.

From the kitchen of
Wally Griffin

Hot Fudge Burger

ground beef
bun
lettuce
onion
tomato
pickles
hot fudge

Make your ground beef into a good sized patty. Grill until done.

Place bun open face on a plate and on the top side of the bun, place lettuce, onion, tomato and pickles.

On the bottom side of the bun place your burger patty. Top the patty with a generous serving of hot fudge.

Enjoy!

Note from Cindy
This was actually on the menu at the restaurant Wally opened in downtown Salt Lake City, Utah. It is where Stuart and I met. I actually served a few of these, but they were only on the menu as a joke. Another recipe that was on that same menu is on page 134.

From the home of
Kacey and Matty Kahler

2 ¼ C self rising flour
2 T cornstarch
½ tsp. salt
¼ tsp. white pepper
1 egg
2 T vegetable oil
1 ¼ C water
1 qt. vegetable oil for frying
8 boneless, skinless chicken breasts, cut into 1" cubes

Crispy Chicken
Deep fried for Asian dishes

Whisk the egg together with the oil and water. Combine flour, cornstarch, salt and pepper. Gradually add the dry ingredients to the egg mix to make a thick batter. Stir to blend thoroughly. Add chicken pieces and stir until chicken is well coated.

Heat oil in a skillet or wok to 360°. Fry chicken pieces in hot oil 10 minutes or until golden brown.

Remove chicken and drain on a paper towel.

Note from Kacey
Great for leftovers. Serve on a sandwich with lettuce, mayo and provolone cheese.

123

From the home of
Stuart and Cindy Eder

5 large eggs
5 - 6 mushrooms, sliced
½ of a sweet onion, chopped
1 T oil
1 C half & half
¼ tsp. salt
½ C shredded cheddar cheese
½ C shredded Swiss cheese
nutmeg

Crustless Quiche

Preheat oven to 350°.

Heat oil in a skillet over high heat and add mushrooms and onions. Sauté until onions are translucent then set aside.

Beat eggs and add half & half. Salt and pepper if desired.

Spray a 9 inch deep dish glass pie pan with non-stick cooking spray. Add the mushrooms and onions. Top with the shredded cheese.

Pour the egg mixture over the cheese. No need to stir.

Sprinkle the top with nutmeg.

Bake for 50 - 55 minutes or until golden brown.

Note from Cindy
Great recipe for those who need to be gluten free.

Quiche Lorraine

1 unbaked pie crust, 9 inch
1 C shredded Swiss Cheese
6 slices cooked bacon, crumbled
¾ C ham, minced
2 green onions, sliced and chopped
½ C green pepper, chopped
3 eggs, beaten
1 C light cream
½ tsp. grated lemon peel
½ tsp. salt
¼ tsp. dry mustard

Preheat oven to 425°.

Bake unbaked pie crust for 5 minutes. Remove from oven and reduce temperature to 325°.

Arrange cheese, bacon and ham in the bottom of pie shell. Sprinkle green onions and green peppers over the cheese.

Combine the rest of the ingredients and pour evenly over the cheese mixture.

Bake for 45 minutes or until egg is set.

From the home of
Jan and Owen Richardson

Sheet Quiche

8 eggs
½ C sour cream
½ C milk
1 ½ C shredded cheese
English muffins, enough to line pan
meat, any kind you like

Preheat oven to 350°.

Whip eggs. Stir in sour cream and milk.

Line a 9 x 13 inch baking pan with upside down English muffins. Pour egg mixture over the muffins.

Top with cheese and meat. Bake until set.

From the kitchen of
Stuart and Cindy Elder

Skirt Steak

Marinade
2 - 3 C water
1 C burgundy
½ C soy sauce
½ C white vinegar
1 tsp. ginger
½ C brown sugar

Glaze
1 C mushrooms, sliced
1 C onions, sliced
½ C green peppers, sliced
¼ C wine vinegar
¼ C soy sauce
¾ C honey
1 ½ quart water
¼ fresh pineapple, sliced thin

House Rice
recipe on page 94

Marinated Skirt Steak
Honolulu Style

Prepare house rice according to recipe found on page 94.

Prepare the skirt steak for marinating by slicing it crisscross halfway through on the top. Turn it over and do the same to the bottom side. Combine all the marinade ingredients together. Place scored meat into the marinade and leave at least 4 hours. Cook to well done on a grill.

Sauté mushroom, onions and peppers, then add the rest of the glaze ingredients. Thicken with corn starch to a glaze, not too thick.

Slice cooked meat into thin strips.

Serve on individual plates. Start with a generous serving of rice and top it with several slices of the meat. Top with a generous amount of glaze.

From the home of
and Matthew Kahler

Velvet Chicken

1 egg white, beaten
1 T soy sauce
1 tsp. corn starch
⅛ tsp. pepper
1 lb. chicken

Mix together the first 4 ingredients and place in a large plastic bag.
Cut the chicken into one inch cubes and place in the plastic bag.

Coat the chicken thoroughly.

Marinate in the fridge at least 30 minutes.

Bring a pot of salted water to a boil and carefully drop in the chicken.
Cook for 3 minutes.

Remove chicken and let dry on a paper towel.

Chicken can be added to stir fry or just pan fry alone and add your
favorite sauce.

From the home of
Jana Elder

Apricot Chicken

4 -5 skinless chicken breasts
1 bottle Russian salad dressing
1 pkg. dry onion soup mix
4 oz. apricot jam

Preheat oven to 350°.

Place chicken in pan. Mix remaining ingredients and pour over chicken.

Bake uncovered for 2 hours.

house rice (recipe on pg. 94)
broccoli
walnuts
mushrooms
onions
sour cream
shredded cheese
olive oil

Walnut Mushroom Casserole

Preheat oven to 350°.

Cook rice according to recipe on page 94. Place on the bottom of a 9 x 12 casserole dish.

Sauté mushrooms and onions in a little oil over high heat until onions are caramelized and then spread them evenly over the rice.

Sauté walnuts in a little oil for a few minutes and spread evenly over the mushrooms and onions.

Steam broccoli for a few minutes until they turn a bright green. Drain water and place evenly over the mushrooms and onions.

Place dollops of sour cream across the top and then shredded cheese on top of that.

Most of the ingredients should still be warm. Bake uncovered for 20 - 30 minutes or until heated through and cheese browns.

Note from Stuart
This is more appealing if you make it in single serving baking dishes and serve it in the dish it is baked in.

Linda's Pot Luck

1 cut up chicken or pork chops
potatoes
carrots
onions
fresh mushrooms
1 can golden mushroom soup
½ stick margarine

Brown meat in margarine. Electric fry pan works well. Cut up vegetables and place around the meat.

Salt and season to taste. Pour soup over everything and add 1 can of water.

Simmer 1 hour with lid on.

Note: The soup makes a nice gravy and everything is in one pan.

Note from Cindy
One of the recipes I got from Aunt Marge.
Published with Linda's permission.

white fish
¼ onion
1 ½ C soy sauce
juice of 3 limes
2 - 3 tsp. mustard

Samoan Raw Fish

Chop the fish into ¾ inch square pieces and drain all the water off.

Put fish in a large bowl and add remaining ingredients. Mix and pour into a large jar. Put the lid on and shake a few times.

Chill and eat when desired.

Note from Marge
Sam taught me to fix this for him and his family. It is
the way it is done in most Samoan homes.

CAKES, PIES & DESSERTS

From the home of
Ella Mae & Walter Griffin

1 C butter
1 C milk
2 C brown sugar
1 quart bread crumbs
1 ½ T baking powder
1 ½ C flour
¾ tsp. baking soda
1 tsp. salt
1 tsp. powdered clove
2 tsp. nutmeg
2 tsp. cinnamon
2 C shredded carrots
2 C shredded apples
2 C raisins
4 eggs
grated nuts and dates to taste

Lemon sauce
¼ pound of butter
2 T cornstarch
2 C water
⅔ C brown sugar
juice of ½ a lemon, rind grated
pinch of salt

Plum Pudding

Sift flour and spices. Add beaten eggs to milk and mix with dry ingredients except baking soda. Dissolve baking soda in hot water, then add to batter.

Add fruits, carrots and nuts to batter.

Grease container (4 cup pudding mold), fill ¾ full and steam about 3 hours or until fork inserted in the middle comes out clean.

For lemon sauce, bring all ingredients to a boil and thicken.

Serve warm with lemon sauce.

Note from Cindy
Thanks to Suzanne Griffin for saving this recipe. The milk amount was not on the recipe so not sure of the exact amount. If memory serves me, Grandma would make this in a large coffee can, covering it with foil and placing the can in a pan of water on the stove. Plum pudding is a traditional British Christmas recipe. I remember Grandma making it for Thanksgiving too.

From the home of
Anna and Ronald Gibby

3 C flour
2 C sugar
2 tsp. soda
3 tsp. cinnamon
½ tsp. salt
1 C nuts
1 ½ C oil
2 tsp. vanilla
1 C pineapple
pineapple juice
3 eggs, beaten
2 C carrots, grated

Frosting
1 small pkg. cream cheese
½ stick of butter
1 tsp. vanilla
½ box confectioners sugar
½ C pecans

Carrot Cake

Preheat oven to 350°.

Mix all ingredients together except pineapple juice. Pour into a greased 13 x 9 inch pan.

Bake for 1 hour.

Glaze with pineapple juice and powdered sugar.   Pour over while hot.

Frosting: Mix first four ingredients together. Frost cake and add chopped nuts to the top.

Note from Debbie
I'm guessing over the years Mom perfected that carrot cake using raisins, coconut and walnuts. Often she would make the mini loafs and pass those out around the holidays to friends and family.

From the home of
Jan and Owen Richardson

Chocolate Sheet Cake

½ C butter
½ C shortening
4 T cocoa
1 C water
2 C flour
2 C sugar
½ C buttermilk
1 tsp. baking soda
1 tsp. cinnamon
1 tsp. vanilla
⅛ tsp. salt

Frosting
½ C butter
4 T cocoa
1 tsp. vanilla
6 T milk
4 C powdered sugar
chopped nuts, optional

Preheat oven to 400°.

In a large bowl. mix the flour and sugar together. Boil first four ingredients. Pour boiled ingredients over flour and sugar. Stir to combine. Add remaining ingredients. Mix well.

Pour mixture into a greased and floured sheet cake pan.

Bake for 30 minutes or longer if the pan is deep.

Frosting: Melt butter. Add cocoa, vanilla and milk. Bring to a boil. Remove from heat and add sugar. Mix well.

Note from Jan
This cake is real good when you use applesauce
in place of shortening.

From the home of
Eliza and Walter Griffin

4 eggs
1 C milk
2 C sugar
½ C butter
2 tsp. baking soda
2 ½ C flour

Cupcakes

Mix and bake in small tins.

There are no more instructions, so good luck with this one.

Note from Cindy
One of the recipes I got from Aunt Marge. She said that it came from
the Comforts Family Guide Cookbook (1915) that Eliza used often.

Zucchini Cake

2 C sugar
3 eggs
1 C oil
2 C grated, peeled zucchini
3 C flour
1 tsp. baking soda
½ tsp. baking powder
2 tsp. cinnamon
½ tsp. nutmeg
¼ tsp. cloves
1 tsp. salt
2 tsp. vanilla
1 C nuts

Preheat oven to 350°.

In a large bowl, mix together the ingredients in the order given.

Bake for about 45 minutes until a toothpick inserted in the center comes out clean.

Mandarin Orange Cake

1 pkg. yellow cake mix (Duncan Hines)
3 eggs
½ C oil
1 medium can mandarin oranges, juice and all

Mix together. Beat 8 minutes and bake according to directions on package.

Mix together all frosting ingredients and serve on top of cooled cake.

Frosting:
1 pkg. vanilla instant pudding
1 med. cool whip
1 small can pineapple and juice

Note from Marge
Recipe taken from the file of Jean Griffin.

From the home of
Marge Ault

1 box of gingerbread mix
#2 can of sliced pineapple
Maraschino cherries

Upside Down Gingerbread

Preheat oven to 350°.

Mix gingerbread according to package instructions.

Use any oven proof 1 ½ quart bowl. Grease it and line the bottom and sides with pineapple. Place a cherry in the center of each pineapple.

Pour the gingerbread mixture over the pineapple.

Bake 1 hour in a 350° oven.

Turn upside onto a plate. Serve warm with whipped cream or whipped marshmallow.

Note from Marge
A fun favorite of mine for parties or special occasions. So easy to do and looks fancy. Cut it at the table for friends to see.

5 - 6 golden delicious apples,
peeled and sliced
1 cube of butter, softened
1 ½ C old fashioned oats
1 C raw brown sugar

Apple Crisp

Preheat oven to 350°.

Peel and cut enough apples to fill a 10 x 10 inch glass baking dish mostly full.

Mix butter, sugar and oats. Knead together and cover the apples. Use plenty.

Bake about 20 minutes or until the apples are just done, not mushy.

Serve warm, topped with real whipped cream.

Note from Cindy
Grandma loved to make this for any family gathering.
She always topped it with real whipped cream
or honey vanilla ice cream.

From the home of
Jan and Owen Richardson

8 C sugar
1 ½ C cornstarch
1 ½ tsp. salt
1 T cinnamon
1 tsp. mace
2 ½ qt. water
1 stick butter
1 lemon rind and juice
apples

Bottled Apple Pie Filling

In large pan, combine everything but the apples. Add raw apples when mixture thickens.

Pour into prepared bottles and seal. Boil 20 minutes.

When you need a pie, just dump straight out of the bottle between 2 crusts and bake.

Cream Cheese Pie

Filling
12 oz. cream cheese
2 eggs, beaten
1 tsp. lemon juice
1 tsp. grated lemon rind
¾ C sugar
2 tsp. vanilla

Crust
13 - 14 graham crackers, crumbled
¼ C melted butter

Topping
1 C sour cream
3 ½ T sugar
1 tsp. vanilla

Preheat oven to 350°.

Make crust by thoroughly combining the cracker crumbs with the butter and pat into a 9 inch pie plate. Set aside.

Combine all filling ingredients and beat until light and frothy. Pour into a graham cracker crust and bake for 25 - 30 minutes.

Remove from oven and allow to cool for 5 minutes.

Blend together the topping ingredients. Pour topping over pie and return to oven for 10 minutes longer.

Place in refrigerator for at least 5 hours before serving. Add a spoonful of strawberry or other flavor jelly to the top of eash slice of pie if desired.

Note from Frances
Dad loved this pie. It is a family favorite.

From the home of
Jan and Owen Richardson

Cream Puffs

4 eggs
1 C boiling water
1 C flour
½ C shortening
½ tsp. salt

Preheat oven to 400°.

Combine shortening, salt and water. Heat to boiling.

Sift and measure flour. Add to boiling mixture. Beat vigorously until mixture leaves sides of saucepan and does not cling to spoon.

Remove from heat. Cool. Add eggs, one at a time. Beat thoroughly after each addition.

Drop by tablespoons in muffin tins or on a cookie sheet.

Bake in hot oven (400°) for 30 minutes. Lower heat to 350° and continue to bake 10 minutes or until firm and dry.

Cut a slit and fill with whipped cream or cream filling.

From the kitchen of
Wally Griffin

vanilla ice cream
hot fudge
chopped nuts
maraschino cherry
whipped cream
cooked chicken, cut in bite size
pieces

Chicken Ripple Ice Cream

Place several scoops of ice cream into a large sundae dish. Insert pieces of chicken into the ice cream.

Top with hot fudge, whipped cream, chopped nuts and place a cherry on top.

Note from Cindy
Another recipe that was on the menu of a restaurant Wally opened in downtown Salt Lake City, Utah. It was meant as a joke but people actually ordered it and brought their friends back the next night and ordered it again. The restaurant was called Paradise Island and it is where Stuart and I met.

Coffee Jelly

2 tsp. unflavored gelatin
¼ C sugar
4 C coffee

Topping:
whip cream
caramel sauce

Make coffee as usual and add sugar.

Chill. Add the gelatin and stir until dissolved.

Freeze in single serving dishes about ¾ full.

Top with whipped topping and caramel sauce before serving.

1 bag milk chocolate chips
1 bag Reese's peanut butter chips
1 box graham crackers
1 small tub cool whip
2 - 3 T peanut butter
miniature marshmallows

Freezer Smores

Place all the chips in a microwave safe bowl. Heat for 30 seconds at a time, stirring in between until all are melted.

Add in the peanut butter and stir to combine.

Add in the cool whip and stir to combine.

Add in the marshmallows. By this time the mixture has cooled enough to not melt the marshmallows.

Line a baking sheet with parchment. Break graham crackers into squares and place on top of the parchment.

Use a small ice cream scoop and place one scoop on each cracker. Place another cracker on top of each one and press down slightly.

Freeze for at least 2 hours. Eat without thawing. Store in a Ziploc bag in the freezer.

From the home of
Jan and Owen Richardson

Fresh Strawberry Pie

1 ½ qt. fresh strawberries
1 C sugar
3 T cornstarch
2 T lemon juice
1 C whipping cream
1 pie shell

Wash the berries. Mash half of them. Add sugar and cornstarch.

Cook over medium heat. Cook until smooth and thick. Stir in lemon juice.

Cool.

Add whole berries and pour in pie crust. Top with whip cream and garnish with a few fresh berries.

Cheesecake

16 oz. cream cheese, softened
1 C sugar
2 eggs
graham cracker crust

Preheat oven to 350°.

Place first 3 ingredients into a bowl and beat until smooth.

Pour mixture into a readymade graham cracker crust.

Bake 30 - 35 minutes.

From the kitchen of
Wally Griffin

Rainbow's End

1 T olive oil
1 apple, cubed
2 oranges, peeled and chopped
1 banana, sliced
2 oz. chopped pecans
1 oz. raisins
4 T honey
¼ tsp. cinnamon
¼ tsp. nutmeg

Add the oil to a sauté pan and get it hot. Add the fruits to the pan, in the order they are listed, sautéing each before adding the next.

When they are sizzling hot, add in the nuts, raisins, honey and spices. Heat until vigorously bubbling.

Serve hot over honey vanilla ice cream.

COOKIES, BARS & CANDY

Applesauce Cookies

1 C shortening
2 C white sugar
4 eggs
4 C flour
2 tsp. baking soda
1 tsp. baking powder
1 tsp. salt
1 tsp. cinnamon
1 tsp. nutmeg
nuts
chocolate chip

Preheat oven to 350°.

Cream sugar and shortening, Add eggs.

Add soda to the applesauce and add to the egg mixture.

Add dry ingredients.

Drop on greased baking sheet and bake for 15 minutes.

Note from Cindy
One of the recipes I got from Aunt Marge.

Aunt Fern's Cookies

1 ⅓ C raisins or currants
¾ C shortening
1 ½ C white sugar
2 eggs, beaten
3 C flour
1 tsp. baking soda
1 tsp. baking powder
1 tsp. salt
1 tsp. cinnamon
1 tsp. nutmeg

Boil 1 ⅓ C small raisins or currants in 1 C water for 5 minutes

Add ¾ C shortening. Cool.

Add in the rest of the ingredients and beat together.

Drop by spoonfuls on baking sheet.

Note: Aunt Fern only oiled the pan once.

Note from Cindy
One of the recipes I got from Aunt Marge.

2 ¼ C flour
2 tsp. ground ginger
¾ tsp. ground cinnamon
½ tsp. ground cloves
¼ tsp. salt
1 tsp. baking soda
¾ C butter softened
1 C sugar
2 T sugar to roll ball in
1 egg
1 T water
¼ C molasses

Big Soft Ginger Cookies

Preheat oven to 350°.

Sift together the dry ingredients and set aside.

In a large bowl, cream together butter and sugar until light and fluffy.
Beat in egg, then 1 cup sugar, water and molasses until well combined.
Gradually stir in the sifted ingredients.

Shape dough into balls and roll them in the 2 T sugar. Place 2 inches
apart on an ungreased cookie sheet and flatten slightly.

Bake for 8 - 10 minutes. Cool on baking sheet for 5 minutes before
transferring them to a wire rack to cool completely.

*Ginger has many medicinal properties. It can be used to
treat nausea, especially morning sickness. It may help with
weight loss, lower blood sugars, improve heart problems
and may help lower cholesterol.*

From the home of
Jana Elder

1 C zucchini, grated
1 tsp. baking soda
1 C sugar
½ C shortening or butter
1 egg, beaten
2 C flour
1 tsp. cinnamon
½ tsp. ground cloves
½ tsp. salt
1 C nuts, chopped
1 C raisins, optional

Zucchini Drop Cookies

Preheat oven to 375°.

Mix together zucchini, baking soda, sugar, shortening and egg.

Sift and stir in flour, spices and salt.

Blend in the nuts and raisins, then drop onto a greased cookie sheet and bake for 12 - 15 minutes.

Makes 3 dozen.

Note from Jana
Zucchini coming out your ears? These are soft and homey. I can't stand to waste good food, so I grill it, make cookies, bread or soup.

½ C butter
½ C brown sugar, packed
¼ granulated sugar
1 egg
1 tsp. vanilla
½ C + 2 T flour
¼ tsp. baking soda
½ tsp. salt
1 ½ C oats
1 C walnuts
1 C semisweet chocolate chips

Chewy Chocolate Chip Oatmeal Cookies

Preheat oven to 325°.

Cream together butter and sugars until smooth. Beat in egg until well combined. Add vanilla extract.

Combine flour, baking soda and salt in a separate bowl, then stir into the creamed mixture just until blended. Mix in the oats, walnuts and chocolate chips.

Drop by heaping spoonfuls onto an ungreased baking sheet and bake for 12 minutes.

Cool on baking sheet for 5 minutes, then transfer to a wire rack to cool completely.

Mint Surprise Cookies

3 C flour
1 tsp. baking soda
½ tsp. salt
1 C butter
1 C sugar
½ C brown sugar
2 eggs, unbeaten
1 T water
2 tsp. vanilla
1 pkg. Rockwood mint chocolate
wafers
walnuts

Preheat oven to 375°.

Sift together flour, soda and salt.

Cream butter, sugar and egg together.

Add eggs, water and vanilla to creamed mixture,

Blend in dry ingredients. Cover and chill for at least 2 hours.

Take a mint chocolate wafer and enclose it in about 1 T chilled dough and top with a walnut half.

Bake for 12 minutes.

Date Kisses

2 egg whites
pinch of salt
1 C powdered sugar
1 C diced dates
½ tsp. vanilla
¾ C chopped nuts

Preheat oven to 325°.

Beat egg whites to a peak. Add salt and vanilla. Add sugar a little at a time with continuous beating.

Add dates and nuts by folding in. Drop in small amounts on a slightly greased cookie sheet.

Bake in a slow oven until slightly tanned.

Note from Cindy
One of the recipes I got from Aunt Marge.

Lake Powell Cookies

⅓ C peanut butter
½ C sugar
½ C brown sugar
1 egg
1 tsp. vanilla
1 ¾ C flour
1 tsp. baking soda
½ tsp. salt
36 chocolate candy kisses

Preheat oven to 375°.

Cream butters and sugars until fluffy. Add egg and vanilla.

Sift dry ingredients. Add to creamed mixture. Mix to blend.

Shape dough into 1 inch balls. Roll in sugar and place on cookie sheet.

Bake for 8 minutes. Remove from oven. Top each cookie with a candy kiss, pressing down firmly until cookie cracks around the edges. Return to oven and bake 2 - 3 minutes longer until golden brown.

Makes 3 dozen.

Note from Cindy
Jan always made these for the annual Lake Powell trip so
they quickly became known as Lake Powell cookies.

From the home of
Owen and Janet Richardson

Nutty Pudding Bars

2 C semi sweet chocolate chips
2 C butterscotch chips
1 jar peanut butter (12 oz.)
1 oz. unsweetened chocolate.
1 C butter
5 T vanilla pudding mix (about
half a small box)
⅓ C evaporated milk
1 tsp. vanilla
2 lbs. powdered sugar
2 ½ C peanuts, coarsely chopped

Combine chocolate and butterscotch pieces, peanut butter and unsweetened chocolate in a pan on low heat and stir until melted.

Spread half of the mixture into a 15 x 10 x 1 inch pan. Chill until set. Let remaining mixture stand at room temperature.

Combine butter, pudding mix and milk in sauce pan and stir to melt butter. Add in the vanilla. Place in large mixing bowl and beat in the powdered sugar until smooth. Spread over chilled layer.

Sprinkle nuts on top and spread the remaining chocolate over it.

Chill until firm.

From the home of
Dorothy and Glenn Hardman

Salted Peanut Chews

1 ½ C flour
⅔ C brown sugar
½ tsp. baking powder
½ tsp. salt
¼ tsp. baking soda
½ C butter, softened
1 tsp. vanilla
2 large egg yolks
3 C miniature marshmallows

Topping
⅔ C corn syrup
¼ C butter
2 tsp. vanilla
1 bag of peanut butter chips (10 oz.)
2 C crisp rice cereal
2 C dry roasted peanuts, coarsely chopped

Preheat oven to 350°.

Lightly spoon flour into measuring cups and level off. Combine first 7 ingredients in a large bowl at low speed until crumbly. Press firmly in the bottom of an ungreased 9 x 13 inch pan.

Bake 12 - 15 minutes or until light golden brown. Remove from oven and immediately sprinkle with marshmallows. Return to oven and bake an additional 1 - 2 minutes. Marshmallows will begin to puff. Set aside to cool.

For topping, combine first 4 ingredients in a large saucepan. Heat until the chips are melted and mixture is smooth. Stir constantly. Remove from heat and stir in cereal and peanuts. Immediately spoon topping over marshmallows and spread to cover.

Refrigerate 45 minutes or until firm. Cut into bars. Makes about 36.

Note from Susan Barker
Mom made these every Christmas without fail.
My kids still make them.

Peanut Butter Fondant

3 C sugar
1 C cream
1 tsp. vanilla
½ C peanut butter

Cook first 3 ingredients to soft ball stage.

Cool and beat.

Add peanut butter. Mix and pour in a pan to cool and slice.

Note from Cindy
One of the recipes I got from Aunt Marge.

medjool dates
raisins
dried figs
prunes
nuts of choice
unsweetened coconut

Date Nut Rolls

Remove the pits from the dates. Use any combination of the first 5 ingredients.

Use a meat grinder that hasn't had meat used in it. Alternate between dates, prunes, nuts, raisins and/or figs. Do as much as you desire. Always make the last pass with nuts as it cleans out all the stickiness and makes the grinder easier to clean.

Squish it all together using your hands and roll into little logs. Roll the logs in the coconut and place a nut on the top if desired.

Variations: Carob powder can be added for a chocolate taste or the balls can be rolled in carob honey candy or dipped in a carob coating.

Note from Cindy
Mom made these every year for Christmas. The ones
that she added peanuts to were always my favorites.

BEVERAGES

Frozen Frappe

5 C water
juice of 4 oranges
2 lemons
1 large can pineapple juice
4 bananas
2 - 4 liters 7-up

Mix sugar and water. Bring to a boil for 2 minutes. Cool.

Blend banana with pineapple juice. Mix all together and freeze for 4 hours.

Take out of the freezer and thaw to slush. Dump half of the mixture into a punch bowl. Add 7-up to taste.

Float a few orange wheels on top. Use rest of mixture when needed.

From the home of
Jan and Owen Richardson

2 C cold skim milk
1 pkg. sugar free strawberry
flavored gelatin
8 oz. plain yogurt
1 C crushed ice
1 large banana cut in chunks

Fruit Yogurt Shake

Combine all ingredients in blender. Blend until smooth.

Makes about 6 servings.

Just Peachy Shake

3 C cold skim milk
1 pkg. sugar free vanilla
instant pudding
2 C fresh peaches or frozen
unsweetened peaches slightly thawed

Pour milk into blender. Add pudding mix and peaches. Cover and blend at high speed until smooth.

Serve at once.

Note: Mixture thickens as it stands.

From the home of
Jan and Owen Richardson

Hot Tomato Drink

1 can V-8 juice
water equal to V-8
beef bouillon equal to V-8
8 - 10 drops Tabasco
2 tsp. horseradish

Heat juice, water and bouillon. Add Tabasco and horseradish.

Serve hot.

INDEX

Notes

Notes

Notes

Notes

Made in United States
Orlando, FL
23 December 2023